Weather

By Katrina Rasbold

Two Books About the Magic of Timing & the Timing of Magic

A Bundle of Weather Witchery (c2014)
and Days and Times of Power (c2013)

ISBN-13: 978-1506140131

ISBN-10: 1506140130

Published by Rasbold Ink

www.rasboldink.com

Cover artwork for *Weather or Not* is based on the artwork of DrEaM-St0cK of Deviant Art. Thank you, DrEaM-St0cK, for sharing your talent on this website and allowing your beautiful work available for other deviants to use without restriction. http://dream-st0ck.deviantart.com/art/Sarah-V-2014-498817539

TABLE OF CONTENTS

WEATHER WITCHERY

DAYS AND TIMES OF POWER

Weather Witchery

By Katrina Rasbold

Published by Rasbold Ink

www.rasboldink.com

Cover artwork for *Weather Witchery* is based on the artwork of Twilightsmuse of Deviant Art. Thank you, Twilitesmuse, for sharing your talent on this website and allowing your beautiful work available for other deviants to use without restriction.

http://twilitesmuse.deviantart.com/art/Finding-Warmth-287771185

INTRODUCTION

This book came about because of a class I scheduled on weather magic. I have worked with weather witching for decades and taught classes on the subject many times before, but I thought I would enjoy learning some new angles to share with my students. When you teach for many years, it is easy to fall into a rut and say the same things repeatedly. You still believe most of the same things you felt were true ten years ago when you started the class, so why not stick to the tried and true?

The answer is because it is FUN to learn new things and the usual banter can get boring. In this case, I had not taught weather magic in quite some time and since my life was transitioning in many ways, I was eager to up my game and learn a few new exciting angles. I surprised me to find little material available on such a fascinating subject! I was even more surprised to see that of the little information out there, much of it was steeped in warnings about the dangers of weather witching. Has weather magic become the new scary story to tell in sacred circles with a flashlight under your chin?

Don't worry, kids. I'm here to help. I feel a bit like the little child who shouted out that the emperor has no clothing when I say that weather witchery is a practical, rewarding, and sacred experience open to any Witch willing to give it a try. Weather is part of nature and as Witches, what are we if not natural beings? Witches meld into the shifts and cycles of the world around us. Part of claiming our own inherent power includes working with the natural elements of Earth, Air, Fire, and Water. There is very little about weather that is not an elemental experience, sometimes to the extreme!

There is a tremendously moving scene in the film, "The Mists of Avalon" in which Vivienne is showing Morgaine how to command the elements. She uses her hands to light a fire and then raises her arms in power to call down the rains. Any baby Witch on earth who watches that scene cheers right along with Morgaine as she says, "Show me, Vivienne! I want to LEARN!" The distinction is that in weather witchery, as with any other kind of magical endeavor, the true power comes in working *with* the elements rather than commanding power *over* them.

The type of magic I teach is about stepping into a symphony of cooperative powers of Nature, of which we are an intricate component. Our spirit is our instrument. The concert is underway long before we get there and continues after we step away. We take our place and begin to play, lending our energy and power to the process of the concert going on around us. The "music" is sweeter and stronger as we play and we are proud to be a part of it. We do not dominate the orchestra. To subdue it for a solo performance would detract from the cooperative harmony of the different tones and pitches. We are pleased to take part in the production and to merge with the beauty of the piece in progress. We are not the magic; we are an important part of the magic.

In this case, we meld with the weather. We learn from it, we draw power from it, and we lend power to it. It is not our outcome or our target. It is our working partner. In this book, we will discuss weather lore, explore how different types of weather affect magical energy, and learn to call in certain types of weather systems. Working cooperatively with the powers of Nature is the most essential blessing of Witchcraft and weather is a welcome part of that dance.

CHAPTER 1 – WEATHER LORE

How fascinating must it have been for early humans to note the changes not only in seasons, but also in day-to-day meteorological occurrences? Would rain, with water falling out of the sky, or hail, large pebbles of ice pelting onto the skin, not have been just the weirdest thing ever? It is fascinating to watch the complete befuddlement of a dog, cat, or even a human toddler that has never encountered snow as they stare at the white stuff on the ground.

As early as 650 B.C., the Babylonians tried to predict short-term weather changes and by 300 B.C., the Chinese developed a calendar with 24 festivals outlined, each specifically associated with a different kind of weather. Around 340 B.C., Aristotle wrote a four-volume text on the weather that, although it contained many critical errors, sustained as the ultimate authority on weather theory for almost two thousand years and was eventually overthrown in the 17th century.

It was not until the 19th and 20th centuries that meteorological study became advanced enough for even marginally reliable weather forecasting and now, we launch and track radiosondes – balloon carried weather instruments with radio transmitters - every twelve hours from hundreds of upper air ground stations all over the world. These devices transmit moisture, temperature, and pressure data back to the above ground air stations for information processing.

With these sophistications such a recent development and the weather so critical to ships, crops, and other means of survival, there is little wonder that so many superstitions and prognostications about the weather exist. For thousands of years, it was a source of tremendous mystery and wonderment.

One of the most popular weather phrasing is:

Red sky at night, sailors' delight. Red sky in the morning, sailors take warning.

This particular lore is old enough to be included in the Bible in Matthew 16. Pharisees and Sadducees are testing Jesus by asking him to show them a sign from heaven and part of his rebuke of their demand for proof says, "When evening comes, you say, 'It will be fair weather: for the sky is red.' And in the morning, 'Today it will be stormy, for the sky is red and overcast.' O [ye] hypocrites, ye can discern the face of the sky; but can ye not [discern] the signs of the times?"

Shakespeare also references the belief in his play, "Venus and Adonis:" *"Like a red morn that ever yet betokened, Wreck to the seaman, tempest to the field, Sorrow to the shepherds, woe unto the birds, Gusts and foul flaws to herdmen and to herds."*

He touches on a tender truth, which is that understanding the weather was a vital survival tool for both the sailor and the farmer. Misjudging a forecast could be disastrous for either field or ship. While we know that water vapor and dust particles in the atmosphere and their movements across the sky in relation to the sun's light is what colors the sky, which they knew is that if the sun looked angry early in the day, the weather would eventually turn ugly.

It is no accident that Groundhog Day falls on February 2nd as it is originally tied to one of our sacred holidays, Imbolc, in its Christianized version called Candlemas.

An old English song says:

If Candlemas be fair and bright,
Come, Winter, have another flight;
If Candlemas brings clouds and rain,
Go Winter, and come not again.

According to an old Scottish saying:

If Candlemas Day is bright and clear,

There'll be twa (two) winters in the year.

Another variation of the Scottish rhyme:

If Candlemas day be dry and fair,

The half o' winter to come and mair,

If Candlemas day be wet and foul,

The half of winter's gone at Yule.

The Germans recited:

For as the sun shines on Candlemas Day,

So far will the snow swirl until the May.

And indeed, it was the Germans who brought the tradition of Groundhog Day to Pennsylvania, where Punxsutawney Phil comes out of his heated burrow and predicts the weather for the coming six weeks. If he sees his shadow (meaning, as above, the weather is "bright and clear"), there will be six more weeks of winter. Of course, by our calendar, it is six more weeks until Spring Equinox regardless, but the implication is of winter weather.

This practice is actually thought to originate from an old Scottish tradition, which puts me in mind of the Simpson's "Whacking Day" celebration, in which the Highlanders would pound on the ground with sticks until a snake came up out of the ground. They would then study the movement of the snake, which told them how much frost remained in the season and in theory, when it was safe to plant their fields.

For the record, the National Weather Service has calculated that Punxsutawney Phil's predictions are accurate around 39% of the time.

If there is thunder in winter, it will snow seven days later.

Thunder in winter is atypical and usually indicates a large dip and a rise in the jet stream. Cold air comes up from the south, replaces the warm air, and lifts it up, causing thunderstorms. When the cold air behind the front settles in, it hangs around for several days. It's not necessary the arbitrarily chosen seven days, but temperatures during that time may lower enough to create snow within the week.

When halo rings the moon or sun, rain's approaching on the run

Since a halo is caused by the refraction of the Sun or Moon's light by ice crystals at high altitude, this is generally a good sign of upcoming precipitation.

Not all traditional weather lore has the backing of science to it...yet, which in no way renders it invalid:

If a rooster crows in the middle of the night, it will rain the following day.

When leaves, especially oak leaves, turn upside down, rain is coming.

Seagull, seagull, sit on the sand. It's never good weather when you're on land.

When windows won't open, and the salt clogs the shaker, the weather will favor the umbrella maker!

When birds nest close to the ground, it will be a hard winter.

Other indicators of a hard winter are: corn husks that are thick and tight, tough apple skins are tough, birds migrating early, squirrels with very bushy tails, plentiful berries and nuts, and bees that nest high in the trees.

Where I live in Grizzly Flats, California, we endure extremely harsh winters and are under threat of snow from October until June. We sometimes receive ten to fifteen feet of snow over a season. The saying here is that we have not had our last snowfall until it snows on the dogwood blooms. It is always a time of tremendous joy up here when the dogwood blooms turn white.

When the wind is blowing in the North, no fisherman

should set forth

When the wind is blowing in the East, 'tis not fit for man

nor beast

When the wind is blowing in the South, it brings the food

over the fish's mouth

When the wind is blowing in the West, that is when the

fishing's best!

A Welsh tradition is that if March comes in like a lion, it goes out like a lamb and if it comes in like a lamb, it will go out like a lion (harsh at the beginning means calm at the end and vice versa).

CHAPTER 2 – WEATHER DEITIES

In absence of scientific knowledge, it was natural for our ancestors to attribute weather phenomenon to the behavior of Gods and Goddesses. Such incredible changes in their world that happened outside of their own control must truly be an act of Deity. Personally, I do not feel that scientific explanations necessarily rule out acts of God, but that's just me.

A Celtic group I worked with in the Dallas-Fort Worth area honored the Aos Sí Sidhe, an Irish fairy race of legend, and when we would call them invariably, they brought the wind when they entered the circle. As soon as our skirts began to dance and we felt the kiss of the East wind on our faces, we knew they had risen up out of the mound homes and were with us. The Banshee or "bean sídhe," is named for the Sidhe, and means "woman of the sídhe." This Irish term is applied to a spirit that wails and cries as a harbinger of a person's death. I have found no reference to anyone else having the same windy experience when inviting in the Aos Sí Sidhe, but in our circle, the Aos Sí Sidhe were the bringers of the wind. Likely, it was through similar sacred moments that other deities throughout history became associated with acts of weather.

The Norse people had Dáinn, Dvalinn, Duneyrr and Duraþrór, who were the four stags of the World Tree, Yggdrasill. These four great deer also represented the four elements and the four seasons.

Egyptian mythology speaks of Amun, God of Creating and the Wind and Shu, God of the Wind and the Air.

In Mayan legend, Pauahtuns were the wind deities associated with the Bacab and the Chaac.

Shinatobe is the Japanese goddess of the winds.

The plural Anemoi were four Greek wind Gods: Boreas was the God of the north wind and of winter, Eurus was God of the unlucky east or southeast wind, Notus was God of the south wind, and Zephyrus ruled the west wind. Poseidon, Triton, and the nymphs were water deities.

The Roman form of the Anemoi were called the Venti.

The Incan Pariacaca was God of water and rainstorms.

The Irish God Manannán mac Lir was a God of the sea. Belisama is Goddess of lakes and rivers, fire, crafts, and light.

In Egypt, Nephthys is Goddess of rivers

In Ancient Greece, lightning came from the God Zeus, ruler of the sky while in Norse mythology, lightning came from Thor, the God of war.

These are just some of the sacred faces people around the world gave to those mighty deities who brought the unexplainable right to their doorsteps.

CHAPTER 3 – THE ETHICS OF WEATHER WITCHERY

When I researched new information for my class, I was surprised to find that most of the information I could locate specific to weather witchery involve warnings not to do it. One claim was that weather magic is so exhausting that a human body would not withstand the effort required to sustain the weather event. Another was that "everything happens for a reason and you could really screw something up by changing the weather." If we live by that principle, we will never work magic at all. The doom and gloom predicted by those who denounce weather witchery holds no more value than those who denounce working weather at all. Do Christians not pray for rain in times of drought? My perspective is that we act as grownups regarding our magic, manage it responsibly, and know our own limits or we do not work magic at all. Magic is not a place for childlike fears and reticence. Magic itself, not just weather magic, requires confidence, competence, and ethical behavior.

Most Witches and Pagans practice under the premise of "As it harms none, do what ye will." This is a brilliant dictate and works well as an overall goal; however, it is not truly practical in literal translation. It is impossible to live in this world and harm none, especially when you consider all of the levels on which harm can occur. Do we draw a line between harming non-sentient creatures and humans? Does inconveniencing someone result in harm? What of the butterfly effect that says we cannot predict the harm that could occur with even the simplest of spells?

The fact of the matter is that regardless of what magic you do, you can harm, even in a minor way. If you do magic to create a parking space at the grocery store, do you cause someone to forget three items on their list because they are compelled to finish shopping early and get their car moved to accommodate you? If you do magic to create a space to merge onto a busy onramp, do you cause a baby to be born on the freeway because you slowed down the vehicle transporting the laboring mother nine cars back? Likewise, if you know the land is parched and needs rain, should you perform an effective rain spell and risk raining out an unknown couple's outdoor wedding they planned in the park for that very day?

If you allow yourself to become enmeshed in the "what ifs" of magic, you will quickly find yourself mired in the immobility of "analysis is paralysis." My way of being in the magical world is to move forward with confidence and trust the process. If what we enact is not meant to be, Goddess and God, The Universe, or whatever you consider the overall Divine Providence will neutralize the energy and things will progress exactly as they should. For all you know, the very act of you casting the spell to change the weather could be a sacred part of what Divine Providence demands. Likewise, if you work weather spells and they are ineffective, then it is your turn to understand that the time for what you desire was simply not right.

CHAPTER 4 – MAGIC FOR EVERY WEATHER

Most people know that they have different feelings around different types of weather. The energy of snowfall or hail or high sun or a thunderstorm can be profound and everyone has his or her own preference of desired weather. When your favorite weather changes occur, utilize those precious moments to maximize your energy flow!

There is a vibration and energy specific to each aspect of Nature's expressions through weather and that unique energy is there for us to channel or store for later use. The three most powerful moments in any weather system is when it first begins, when it climaxes, and when it ends. Those pivotal moments create the container for the magical presentation that particular weather movement brings to us.

RAIN

Petrichor is the word for the smell of rain on dry earth and the smell of dust after a rain. It comes from the Greek word "petros," which means "stone" and "ichor," which means the "golden blood of the Gods." The word was created in 1964 by Australian chemists Isabel Bear and R.G Thomas, who made a concerted study of what causes the distinct and often appreciated smell of rain.

There is little doubt that rain is essential to life. Without it, life would not exist on planet earth. We think of amniotic fluid as the water of life and the flow of rushing water conveys great power. In times of drought, not only do we suffer economically and ecologically, but we also suffer emotionally and spiritually. Most people require a balance of water to dry in order to thrive. Since our bodies are composed of water to such a high degree, we homeopathically relate to the humidity and water around us. Many people, even those who do not swim, are drawn to the water and enjoy standing in the ocean or in a river, just to participate with the kinship that exists between humans and water.

The human spirit responds well to percussion and the rhythmic sound of rainfall and thunder tends to awaken a primal energy within us. The element of water is associated with emotion, so it evokes a number of different emotions in us when it falls all around our homes and our bodies. Water also relates strongly to intuition, instincts, and psychic sensitivity.

In moderate amounts, rain soothes and gently cleanses, renewing the land and our spirits with it. In quantity, it carries away all that is weak and extraneous and soaks into the earth to fortify and renew the life it sustains. The energy of rain is effective for second chances and clearing away the old, extraneous debris from your life.

If you want to cleanse a magical working tool, provided, of course, that is it water resistant, place it out in natural rainfall for a little while, visualizing that this gift from the heavens is washing away any energies you do not wish to have present in the tool.

When it is raining outside, do not overuse your left-brain if you can avoid such activity. It is often a struggle to focus on analytical and academic matters when surrounded by water, which contains the full essence of right-brain experiences. If your schedule allows for it, use rainy days for divination and oracle reading, for daydreaming and even napping to induce lucid dreaming. Write in your journal. Craft or pursue other creative tasks that do not involve heavy thinking and strategizing.

Run into the rain and stretch out your arms, and imagine the drops are blessings raining down upon you. Blend into the energy of relief and nourishing pleasures that the earth is emitting as it soaks up its own form of mother's milk. As you feel the plants and trees coming back to life again, imagine the life soaking into you as you are reborn. Let the rain slide down your clothing and your body and carry with it what no longer serves you, sluicing it neatly away to ground into the Mother Earth.

Water is attuned to the west, which is the homeland of endings and successful completions. The west leads to the place between the worlds, where we slip between the veils that separate us from other dimensions. Like the dreamy, disconnected mental state we enter when we give into the power of rain, the west shifts our perception and takes us into our Higher Selves. Rainy days are wonderful for astral travel, Shamanic work, and meditation.

SNOW

The first snowfall can be very peaceful and soft. It represents unity because while each snowflake is unique, they work together to create an impact. In fact, French philosopher Voltaire wrote, "No snowflake in an avalanche ever feels responsible." Snowflakes are the perfect reflection of the concept of the microcosm and the macrocosm. We even refer to snow as "snow" whether it is one flake or a huge snowball. Snow globes are popular decorative items because of how strongly we relate to the images inside them of tiny bits of snow drifting onto tranquil scenery.

As every schoolchild accurately knows, every snowflake is uniquely different. Although ultimately improvable, experts are in agreement that it is highly unlikely that any two snowflakes are alike. In her book, *Ice: The Nature, the History, and the Uses of an Astonishing Substance*, author Mariana Gosnell, cites scientist Charles Knight from the National Center for Atmospheric Research in Boulder, Colorado, who estimates there are 10,000,000,000,000,000,000 water molecules in a typical snow crystal. Gosnell comments, "The way they can arrange themselves is almost infinite." She goes on to say that senior climatologist with Environment Canada, David Phillips, estimates that the number of snowflakes that have fallen on Earth over the course of time is 10 followed by 34 zeros.

That is a lot of snow with each individual piece theorized as unique. That is big magic and one hell of a metaphor.

Because of how light refracts from it, our eyes see snow as white. In fact, in heavy snowfall, nearly all we see is white to the point that people become "snow blind" in some blizzards. Snow conceals and masks everything it touches in a coat of white. White represents purity, innocence, and freshness. The adage "As pure as the driven snow" identifies this concept.

White and therefore, snow, are associated with the Moon and specifically, the Full Moon which brings revelations and awareness. Even though snow is sneaky and coats everything so that the true nature is unseen, it brings inner awareness. The Moon is the same way. Moonlight is tricky and can turn a pile of clothing on a chair into a slumbering monster. The Moon speaks to our inner seeing and like rain and the west, addresses the places between the worlds where truths beyond our practical world lie.

Quartz crystal is also white to clear, just like snowflakes, and both snow and quartz hold similar qualities. Both conduct energy exceptionally well, so magic worked during times of snow redoubles.

The attribute of purity and freshness associated with snowfall provides fantastic energy for clear thinking and hitting the reset button on difficult situations. The concealment snow provides allows us to see things in a new way and from a different perspective, much again as does the Moon.

The fact that tiny, individual pieces come together to create a huge production that we refer to as snowfall creates the perfect energy for working magic of cooperation and unity.

Snow is stealthy and nearly silent. Here in the mountains of California where I live, we have plenty of opportunity to interview snow and yes, it does make a sound as it falls, but you have to listen to catch it. We can go to sleep with green grass in the front yard and while we slumber, several feet of flaky white can dump on our home and grounds without us even realizing it. This means that times of snow are also conducive to magic involving covert or secret activities that happen away from the awareness of others. As before, the fact that snow covers everything is also good energy for keep secrets and hiding situations from view.

Another important aspect of snow is that it tends to fall in the winter, which is an intensely female time of the year. Winter Solstice is traditionally the height of female power and Summer Solstice is the height of masculine power. Feminine energy is internal and receptive like the winter and masculine energy is projective and external like the summer. Winter related weather, such as snow and hail, tend to carry female attributes while summer weather conditions are primarily masculine.

WEATHER OR NOT By Katrina Rasbold

Whenever I see snow falling, I always hear Tchaikovsky's Nutcracker Suite playing in my head. The delicate fall stirs the magic inside me profoundly and I get a little breathless from it. That comes from someone who despises the inconveniences snow presents. I hate driving in the snow and so I am often landlocked for weeks or even months out of the year as a result. When I was a mail carrier in our town, I had to climb over five and six foot tall berms of snow to get to the mailboxes I had to reach. No, I am not a fan, but as I previously stated, the most powerful moments in a weather front's timing is the very beginning, the climax, and the end. In this case, the beginning evokes tremendous power and the magic is nearly palpable as those first flakes begin to fall from the sky.

As with the rain, go out into the snow as it begins to welcome it and accept its blessings. Feel the uniqueness of every flake that falls and compare it to your own singularly special spirit that is completely impossible to duplicate throughout all of time and every dimension. Close your eyes and imagine that all of your insecurities, all of your fears, and all of your obstacles are disappearing under the blessed, sacred, coat of purity that falls from heaven all around you.

Go to a solid surface like your car's windshield and as the snow covers it completely, write your wish with your finger, then allow the snow to fill in the empty gaps you created and take your words to the Goddess. See the mantle of white as Her arms wrapping around you and your entire world, taking you away into a place where you are safe and protected.

HAIL

Hail is strong and full of intention. When it speaks, people listen. It varies in size, so its impact is flexible to the circumstances. Any type of weather can be destructive in excess. The bright Sun can burn us. Rain can create flooding. Snow can crush homes, cause vehicle accidents, and bring other health hazards. Lightning can burn or electrify. Great winds can be destructive.

Hail, however, has a particular edge to it that other types of weather do not possess. It is easy to slip into the idea that hail is always angry because of its incredible aggression. Many humans tend to shy away from confrontation and "in your face" behavior and hail is nothing if not insistent.

Because of our resistance to confrontation, the energy of hail can infuse us with strength and persistence. If we feel reticent or we need to address a situation we are actively avoiding, hail can give us the boost we need to take action. Hail has the kick-in-the-pants many of us need to motivate us out of an uncomfortable place that is familiar to us, yet also detrimental to our progress. We usually are quite aware that change needs to happen, but we fill our minds and our world with excuses and reasons why we do not move forward despite signs of urgency that we must.

When it begins to hail, most people get up and move. They go inside, even if they stayed outside for rain or snow moments before. Hail gets our attention and it does so through pain. A sad fact is that pain of some type is the primary motivator for change in humans.

Hail rarely lasts for very long. It comes in hard, showers down its message, and then is gone just as quickly, returning to rain or snow. When you first begin to hear the tattoo of hail beating on your roof, hear it as the Goddess knocking at your door insistently. She is trying to get your attention and tell you, "Now, now, *now*. We have to MOVE!"

The magic of hail is urgent and intense, just like the hail itself. There is no time to waste when it comes. Hear Her knock and as quickly as possible, find a few moments to yourself. You are receiving an urgent message from the Goddess, so put everything on hold. Empty your mind to everything except the sound of the hail. Take several deep breaths and focus your attention on *that thing* you always avoid. Without preamble or hesitancy, confront the thing you do not want to see, do not want to feel, and push away in your everyday life. In this one, sacred moment, you have the strength to manage it. That is the message of the hail. Tap into the rhythm of the hail that is falling and step boldly into your own confidence. Become one with the ferocity and the tenacity of the hail and without giving it much thought, make a plan. If you have pen and paper nearby, start writing out your plan. Work on it for as long as the hail falls, then you are done. Within the words you have written, you have tied the power of the hailstorm.

Once the hailstorm is over and you have the beginning of your plan in place, do not be afraid to ask for help. Remember the nature of hail. There is not just one hailstone that falls from the sky, but thousands. Hail speaks to the concept of "strength in numbers." Assemble a team of trusted helpers and advisors to brainstorm with you and keep you motivated. Hail tells you that you have resources you do not yet even recognize.

Hail assures you that you have tremendous strength that you do not fully use to your own advantage. Heed the call and make the change you know you need to make. The gift of hail brings you into stark awareness that what you want and need counts and that the timing is correct to make your move.

THUNDERSTORMS

The call to action that hail brings is demanding, there is no doubt, but the mighty majesty of a thunderstorm is undeniable when the wind, rain, thunder, and lightning really start to kick. Nature is speaks forcefully in several different language at once, creating a time of intense energy and fierce power. In this case, the climax of the storm brings the highest energy, even though the beginning and the tapering off hold nearly as much strength.

Our first three weather conditions, rain, snow, and hail, all have one thing in common: water. Inherently, their energy draws back to the power of water and the west. The crescendo of power from thunderstorms comes from the fact that they possess strong energy from all four elements at once. Thunder relates to earth, lightning is affiliated with fire, rain is – of course – water, and the wind is the essence of air. A true thunderstorm whips all four of the elements into a frenzy and imbues the environment with their strongest attributes.

It is easy to see the male or female energies of meteorological events when we consider them in terms of the element they represent. Water and Earth are the two elements assigned female attributes in nature and Fire and Air are male. This means that wind, lightning, and high

30

sun are masculine events while rain, snow, thunder, and hail are feminine. Not only does a thunderstorm perfectly blend all four elemental energies, but it also perfectly combines and balances male-female energies.

This means that a thunderstorm is the blank check of weather magic. You can use it for very nearly any magical work, cranked up to high amperage. If the storm comes up unexpectedly, then the magic is even stronger. Like the hailstorm, it calls you to work here and now. The freak thunderstorm calls your attention to an important work and everything else needs to take a back seat for at least a few minutes while you do that thang you do.

If you are comfortable going out into the storm and can do so safely, direct exposure will bring your strongest magical results. Otherwise, position yourself so that you feel as much of the storm as possible, such as opening doors and windows, turning off lights, and eliminating distractions in the areas such as computers, TVs, radio, etc. Allow yourself to focus on all of the sounds and sensations of the storm.

Count the breaths between the thunder and the lightning and gauge the approach and retreat of the storm. Let your energy build with the storm and diminish as the storm moves away from you.

As the storm approaches, send your mind out and find the heart of it. See it swirling and moving, alive with power and pulsing with energy. Reach into the heart of the storm and begin pulling it close to you. The more you become one with the energy of the storm, the easier this will be to do. Create an exchange with the storm wherein you give your energy into it and it pours its essence into you.

Close your eyes and let the storm flow through you. Become one with the wind and if possible, allow the rain to wash over you. Let the thunder become your insistent, strong heartbeat. Breathe very deeply and regularly, taking in the scents of the storm and the humidity and ozone it brings. Feel your skin begin to tingle as the energy flows through you and around you.

Direct the energy of the storm toward the magical goal that is most prominent in your life at that time. Feel the energy of the storm begin to move around that goal, investigating it, studying it, evaluating it. Externalize your goal and give it to the storm. Feel the release as it leaves you and goes into the heart of the storm. Let the storm work on it, infusing it with change and with resolution. See the goal begin to glow and to move as if it is alive. See it contort and change as the storm works on it.

As the storm begins its retreat and the intensity diminishes, release your connection to the heart of the storm and to the goal that you placed into it. Slowly pull your own energy back into you and allow the goal to move away from you, knowing that it will come back resolved and perfected. Most importantly, do not revisit the goal for at least one full moon cycle (28 days). Let it go and let the storm do its work.

HIGH SUN

Hot days may not seem like much of a weather phenomenon, but they bring with them their own intensity and therefore, their own magical power. The closer we get to Summer Solstice, the stronger the male energy grows. Because high heat originates from the Sun, which is a masculine celestial sign and from Fire, which is a masculine element, High Sun energy instills us with the strongest male energies.

Words that go along with an infusion of male energy are

- *warrior*

- *strength*

- *endurance*

- *pro-activity*

- *intensity*

- *projective*

- *analytical*

- *objective*

- *virility*

That is never to imply that women cannot also embody those traits anymore than men cannot also be intuitive, nurturing, healing, life affirming, mystical, or any of the female attributes. We are all beings with both masculine and feminine attributes.

On either side of the Summer Solstice, in the waxing or the waning of the height of male energy, we can have long, blistering hot days. Since the dawn of time, humans have worshipped the Sun as a life source and powerful deity. There is nothing like seeing the Sun break through the clouds after days of rain and gray skies. Before there were alarm clocks and electric lighting, the light of the Sun told us when to wake up and when to go to sleep. The absence of the Sun from the sky during an eclipse was a profound magical event in times gone by.

The power of the Sun is profound and so as with our other weather events, this is a power that we can use in our magic.

We all have times of vulnerability and weakness and the pick-me-up energy of a burst of sunlight is quite a boost.

Choose a yellow or orange stone, even a flat glass marble, and lay it out in the direct sunlight, allowing it to absorb the rays and the heat of the Sun. Once it has collected energy for a few hours, take it inside and place it on your personal altar or put it somewhere safe for future use. When you know that a situation is coming that will require you to exhibit endurance, strength, intensity, or effective strategy beyond what you normally possess, carry that stone with you knowing that it contains the energy of the Sun to bless you and fuel your efforts.

Use the long days of summer much as our ancestors did before us. For all of the medical advances we now possess, ancient people knew a secret to healthy life that we do not now employ. They followed the cycles of Nature in their lives rather than continuing the same level and type of productivity throughout the entire year. Consider the harvest cycle. They planted and fertilized in the spring, nurtured and protected in the summer, harvested in the fall, and then rested and planned in the winter. They used the long days of the summer months to put in some of their hardest physical work and then went inside and used the introspective, feminine time of the year to plan and learn.

In our modern life, we tend to demand the same level and type of productivity with no shift to accommodate the changing seasons and the cycles we go through internally that reflect those natural transitions. Just as our bodies and minds are meant to rest in the winter, we are meant to be active and engaged in the summer.

High Sun days are great for motivational magic to build stamina, strength, and aggression in ourselves (or in others!). When the Sun is high and hot, our magic can light a fire under a situation, stimulate it, and get it moving again.

HURRICAINES, TORNADOS, AND OTHER EXTREME SPORTS

It is important to know that any of the four elements that express themselves through weather occurrences can harm us when they are in the height of their power. Each person must weigh out the risks of engaging strong weather conditions and decide where the line between optimum energy and reckless behavior lies. There is no shame in wisely shielding oneself from the harm these extreme weather situations can present.

I have never worked as a professional storm chaser, but I have engaged some heavy-duty weather events and so far, emerged unharmed. I have experienced major earthquakes, tornadoes, floods, and typhoons with coconuts blowing past me, roofs tearing off carports, and power lines dropping around me. I revel in extreme weather and love to feel the power of it coursing through me.

If, like me, your drive is to step right out in the action and take on that energy, it is important to follow some basic safety precautions.

Always let someone know where you will be.

Do not engage lightning if there are cloud-to-ground strikes within a mile of you.

Never stand in the path of oncoming rotating wall clouds or tornados.

Rotating rain curtains, called "the bear's cage," are often immediate precursors for tornado formation, so if you begin to see the rain turn around you, it's time to leave.

Never stop looking around and *up* as well. You must be very aware of your surroundings rather than fixating on one part of the storm.

Do not stand directly in rising floodwaters. They can go "flash flood" faster than you can imagine.

If you are in a lightning storm, avoid touching metal objects and try not to be the tallest target around.

There is great power in extreme storms and yes, the risk involved is part of that high energy. Again, one must always balance out the risks with the benefits.

CHAPTER 5 – HOW TO HARNESS THE ENERGY

As you see from the break down in Chapter 3, the energy of each individual weather type is specific and fuels magic in a powerful way. But what if a weather event is happening and you do not need the energy it provides? One option is to enjoy it for the natural wonder it is and there is nothing at all wrong with that. Another option is to capture the essence of the energy for later use when you *do* need it.

In addition to meteorological occurrences, these two effective techniques can capture the energy of phases of the moon, eclipses, sabbats, or any other type of high-energy moment. To learn more about those, check out my book *Days and Times of Power*, which details specific times and days that add power to magical processes.

KNOT MAGIC

[Please note that this technique may be used to capture the energy of the "Days and Times of Power" identified in the following book in this bundle. This chapter was originally included in that book as well, but has been deleted from the bundle to avoid repeating the information. Use the technique below to contain the energy of solar and lunar events in the same way you would work with a weather event.]

To harness a particular energy for later use, one very effective technique is knot magic. This is an energy storing technique is very effective and requires no more than some intense focus and a length of string or cord the length of the distance from your elbow to your longest fingertip. It should be strong enough that it does not break as you pull on it. It can be of any substance that feels nice in your hands and moves smoothly through your fingers as you tie it off.

Similar to praying the rosary, you will instill your own intent into each "bead," which is actually a knot.

Place yourself as close to the weather occurrence as you safely can. Preferably, you can feel the effects, through an open window or door or if safety allows, in the weather itself. Engage the sensory perception of the event through all five senses as much as you possibly can.

The ideal timing is to begin your knot magic before the weather peaks and follow it over the climax into the descent. You will see that the spellwork itself has a script that creates and entire working ritual based on the progression of the knots.

Hold the cord in your hands and feel yourself tuning into the weather. Become acutely aware of the sounds, the smells, the way your skin feels, the temperature, and the sensations the weather creates. As the weather builds, tie off a knot each time you say a line of the following:

By knot of one, the work's begun (tie the first knot)

By knot of two, I hold it true (tie the second knot)

By knot of three, I bind to me (continue with each knot)

By knot of four, the power I store

By knot of five, it stays alive

By knot of six, the seal is fixed

By knot of seven, from earth to heaven

By knot of eight, I lock the gate

By knot of nine, the power will shine

By knot of ten, I bind within.

When you tie your tenth knot, use it to tie one end of the cord to the other to bring it into a circle, which now binds in the energy of the weather for future use. You can release the energy by untying each knot in a serial release or by burning the cord to release it all at once.

MAGIC WATER

Water is extremely receptive to energy flow, which is why it is such a great conductor of electricity. Find an interesting bottle that seals and fill it with water. Ideally, it is water from a living stream, but water from your tap will work just fine. Set it out, open, in a place that has optimal access to the weather event and leave it there for the duration of the event. Seal it up and it will contain the energy of the weather it experienced.

CHAPTER 6 - HOW TO CALL THE WEATHER

Weather spells are as old as the weather itself. You likely heard one of the easiest and most commonly used ones as a child:

Rain, rain, go away
Come again another day
Little Johnny wants to play
Rain, rain go away.

PULLING IN A SYSTEM

The best way to encourage a weather event is to first find an existing one and then draw it to you with sympathetic or imitation magic. This involves looking at a radar and locating a weather system. The degree of effort required is going to depend on, of course, the likelihood of the weather occurring naturally. Creating a snowstorm from scratch in July yes, would likely kill a person from exhaustion before they actually made it snow. Manifesting a major weather change is much easier if the possibility already exists.

Look on the radar of cities or states near you and see if there is any weather similar to what you desire around

43

you. This can be precipitation or a nice clear, sunny patch or warm and cold fronts to create wind. If you see it, you can usually pull it your way with some heavy visualization. If you do not see it, it is best to wait a day or so and try again.

ELEMENTAL BLAST

As mentioned before, weather experiences are extremely elemental in nature and usually involve a predominance of one or more of the natural elements. It would be foolish to enter into a magical weather-working spell and ignore this vital component. Be certain to honor the elements strongly involved in the weather you wish to manifest and take the time to invoke them into your process.

IMITATION MAGIC

Imitation spell work is the best and easiest kind of weather work. Those famous Native American rain dances often involved different types of imitation spells.

How would you do this? By simulating the experience you wish you have. If you want it to rain, scatter rice onto the ground to simulate raindrops. Dip a broom or a branch in water and sprinkle it over the earth as you visualize. Toss your garden hose and sprinkler onto your roof, turn it on so you see the impression of rain outside your window, and imagine that it is actually raining. Play an MP3 or CD of a rainstorm and hear the sounds to get you in tune with the energy. Use a rain stick as you meditate and visualize, convincing yourself that the tiny seeds inside are actual rain. We know this type of magic is effective because everyone knows the best way to get it to rain is to wash your car, which simulates rain on your vehicle!

If you want wind, use a fan to simulate the sensation.

Drumming mimics thunder and is an excellent way to draw in a storm.

SYMPATHETIC MAGIC

Sympathetic magic means involving scents and tastes that evoke the energy of the weather you seek. Research what herbs are sympathetic to water or wind. If you want to manifest rain, eat juicy, watery foods. Burn incenses made from the herbs that support the weather you want to bring in or sprinkle those herbs onto the ground.

VISUALIZATION

When I speak of meditation and visualization, know that you possess no greater magical tool. Done effectively, visualization takes you into the coveted Delta brain wave where the highest magic takes place. Chanting can induce this, but so can deep mediation. Go heavily into the sensations you create with the simulation magic and take yourself into a deep visualization level. Convince yourself

45

that what you feel is the real thing, that you have manifested this, and that it is a done deal. Sit with it for a while and revel in it.

A common use of visualization is when you need a temporary dry spell in an otherwise rainy day. Perhaps you have some kind of outside activity planned that will be more comfortable if it is not raining. Imagine our surprise when we woke up the morning of Beltane 2014 and found our circle area under several inches of snow! It is tough to get the heat of a passionate maypole rolling when you are shuffling through snow to do it! You can believe a whole circle of Witches started working on creating a sunny sky to melt it all away and guess what? It did!

Here are actual before and after photos to show you it can work:

We simply pushed the snow away using visualization alone and imagined a bright ray of sun shining on our circle area, warming it and clearing away the snow.

SAMPLE WEATHER SPELL

Let's say you want to create my own favorite weather event, a thunderstorm. Here is how I would proceed.

I would first check the radar and locate any storm systems I might be able to pull my way. If one is there, I will give its location a mental bookmark so I can pull it toward me as the ritual proceeds.

Using a standard circle arrangement of four quarters, I would put a chair in the crosshairs at the middle of the circle.

After casting, starting in the North quarter, I would pick up a drum and being to beat a rhythm that mimicked thunder. I would do this for several minutes, then say, "Powers of the North, Element of Earth, I ask that you bring thunder to my storm!" I would then drum a bit longer, until it feels appropriate to move on.

(Please note that in my tradition, energy within the circle moves counter-clockwise)

I would then go to the West quarter, pick up a tree branch or decorative broom I placed there, and dip it into a bucket of water. I would use the broom or branch to flick water drops all over myself and the surrounding area, imagining it to be rain. I would do this several times until the water is gone.

I would then say, "Powers of the West, Element of Water, I ask that you bring rain to my storm!"

I would then move on the South quarter and light a large candle, then watch it for several minutes. When I felt moved to do so, I would say, "Powers of the South, Element of Fire, I ask that you bring lightning to my storm."

I would then move to the East quarter, pick up a fan, and begin to dance with it, swirling my skirts and feeling the wind move around me. When I tired, I would say," Powers of the East, Element of Air, I ask that you bring wind to my storm."

At that time, I would sit in the chair in the center of what I have invoked. I would light an incense that is sympathetic to water and scatter some of it around the chair where I am seated. Next, I eat a juicy orange and play a CD with sounds of a thunderstorm on it while I put my head back, close my eyes and visualize not only the storm, but pulling the storm front that I know exists closer to me.

When I felt the energy was complete, I would thank the elements, close the circle, and let the magic rest, knowing my part was completed.

Notice that the above spell uses imitation magic, sympathetic magic, calls an existing storm front, invokes the elements into the process, and uses visualization. By incorporating all of these different components into the ritual, you bring your heavy hitters into the ballgame in addition to your own personal magic.

CHAPTER 7 – IN CONCLUSION

As with any magical practice, weather witchery is best left to individual preference and need. If you feel your life benefits by interacting with the weather in a magical way, I can personally endorse the activity. In thirty plus years of working in Craft, I have not seen a negative outcome from thoughtful, ethical weather witchery. Sitting outside and pulling a rain cloud toward me is a delightful experience I have enjoyed on many occasions. Creating a sunny opening in an otherwise rainy day to allow us to walk between the raindrops and enjoy a ritual without the rain dousing us served me well more times than I can count.

The combination of deep visualization, imitation magic, and sympathetic magic is usually quite effective for manifesting weather or, for that matter, anything else. Be bold in your magic, but not foolish. Dig deep and challenge yourself, knowing that as long as you work within ethical guidelines, with a pure heart and good intention, your magic will thrive.

Blessed Be.

REFERENCES

Feature, K. (n.d.). Weather and Joint Pain: What's the Link? Retrieved November 15, 2014, from http://www.webmd.com/pain-management/features/weather_and_pain

Gosnell, M. (2005). Ice: The nature, the history, and the uses of an astonishing substance. New York: Knopf.

Groundhog Day History. (n.d.). Retrieved November 16, 2014, from http://www.groundhog.org/groundhog-day/history/

Infocloud | Snow. (n.d.). Retrieved November 16, 2014, from http://qi.com/infocloud/snow

"No Two Snowflakes the Same" Likely True, Research Reveals. (n.d.). Retrieved November 16, 2014, from http://news.nationalgeographic.com/news/2007/02/0702 13-snowflake_2.html

Sixteen Lakota Mysteries in Main Reference Library Forum. (n.d.). Retrieved November 17, 2014, from http://spiritlodge.yuku.com/topic/504#.VGlSPfnF_0c

Weather Forecasting Through the Ages : Feature Articles. (n.d.). Retrieved November 16, 2014, from http://earthobservatory.nasa.gov/Features/WxForecastin g/

Weather Lore Calendar. (n.d.). Retrieved November 15, 2014, from http://www.almanac.com/content/weather-lore-calendar

Days and Times
of Power
A Guide to Optimizing High Energy
Solar and Lunar Moments

PART OF THE BIO-UNIVERSAL ENERGY SERIES

By Eric & Katrina Rasbold

Days and Times of Power

By Eric and Katrina Rasbold

Our cover for *Days and Times of Power* features the beautiful artwork of San Jaya Prime on Deviant Art:

http://jayaprime.deviantart.com/

Chapter 1 – Why Are Certain Days and Times Important?

In human life, we choose certain days to celebrate particular feelings and events. As we move from culture to culture, those days shift and greatly reflect the values upheld by the particular society concerned. We celebrate anniversaries of important happenings, including our own birth. We have holidays that are of religious significance to us and connect us deeply to our own version of what is divine and sacred, as well as to the traditional stories that link us together on a spiritual level.

All of these days have one particular underlying theme and that is the directed focus of many, many people on one particular thought process. This is a tremendously powerful experience and is not to be taken lightly. In our exploration of the many ways in which people seek out The Divine, we have never failed to be impressed by the incredible force of group focus. Not only does it affect the people who are directly involved, but over a period of hundreds or even thousands of years, the repeated act of investing into a particular time period or day by a large number of people creates a collective consciousness response to that particular time period or day.

So profound is this effect that even multiple spiritual paths have felt the significance of particular days and times. There is a huge "who came first?" movement in the observation of certain holidays and the adaptation incoming religions placed onto existing practices. Although we can be assured that manipulation and political malice was actually involved in the reconstruction of ancient holidays into more palatable appearances that better served the incoming regime, to some degree, we think that it was the historical pull of those particular moments that prevented the political forces from simply moving their holidays to a different time.

The majority of the holidays observed in our society have their roots in the ancient agricultural practices. When we discovered that we could grow our own crops, we stopped being nomadic people and began to establish villages and governments. The focus of these united groups of people rested on four things: defeating other villages and government in war, establishing and maintaining profitable trade, hunting and preservation of meat, and the health and vitality of the harvest. Whole villages depended on the success of the harvest for their very survival. Likewise, if what they needed to live could not be grown, they could likely trade what they did grow for what they needed. If the harvest failed, survival was not assured. If they were not successful in their hunts, survival was not assured.

Winters were harsh and without proper sustenance, the weak and sometimes the strong would not live. People watched as natural disasters took out their harvests in a day. They noticed that in some Winters, game was plentiful and fell easily. In other Winters, none was to be found. They attributed this spectrum of success or failure to the will of the Gods. They also created a cycle of celebrations designed to please the Gods and assure the success of the harvest. Some of these celebrations were based upon observable solar phenomena such as the solstices and the equinoxes. Others were related to the behavior of their crops and livestock, such as the birth of the first lambs.

In our modern technological age, it is hard for us to imagine a time before the Industrial Revolution when life did not center on what factories could produce. Yet for thousands of years, life proceeded in this fashion. Because so many people in cultures around the world acknowledged these specific cycles, the practice became embedded in our own collective consciousness and remains there today. Just as the instinct of "fight or flight" is still strong within us even though our time as predator and prey is long past for most of us, so does the call of the eight agricultural holidays still resonate with us though they no longer govern our activities on a wide scale. We still feel new beginnings in the Springtime. Our outdoor physical activity increases during the Summer. We celebrate harvest and our blessings in the Fall. We seek to be close to our families and share togetherness in the Winter.

In our modern application, to honor the eight agricultural holidays is to harness the energy and practices of literally millions of people over thousands of years of human existence. As humans, we are still attuned to the rhythm of that cycle and when we purposely put ourselves into that cycle, we are able to better access that energy and put it to work in our lives. Using this energy, we can "harvest" positive manifestation in our lives

While the progression of the seasons describes a process throughout the solar year, the Moon... Ah, the Moon... She is a whole other force at work in our lives. On a monthly basis, the Moon moves through her phases, lending a detailed energy into all that we do. The Moon is the celestial representation of change and of continuity. It leaves; it comes back. Always waxing and waning; Shakespeare's inconstant orb.

Using those two Heavenly bodies, we are able to guide our energy work in a practical way that eases into the long-existing patterns to better support the goals we wish to make manifest.

Chapter 2 - The Power of the Sun

Assigned to them by people over the ages, the planets, the Moon, and the Sun have a particular energy to them. The Sun is strong, aggressive, and omnipresent. This caused people over time to think of it as a masculine energy. Many cultures since the tracking of time began have worshiped the sun for its life sustaining qualities.

In astrology, the Sun represents the foundation on which our personality is built. The planet that is coming over the horizon at the moment of our birth is the house we build on the foundation of the Sun for all to see. The Moon is the interior of our soul that we use to furnish the house and that only a few will see.

The Sun moves through twelve signs in a year's time. They each have their own energy to lend. The moon moves through those same signs as well, in addition to the phases of New (Dark Moon), Full, Waxing, and Waning.

All of these contribute energy toward what we do every day and they certainly can be a tremendous asset to our energy flow if we learn how they influence our daily lives.

Other astrological forces can be used to accentuate your efforts by nature of their characteristics. Aries is a very assertive sign. Taurus loves creature comforts. Virgo is very organized. Gemini thinks quickly. Learn the positive qualities of the Sun and Moon sign in which you are working and call on their influence to accentuate your magical work.

The sign the Sun is in at the time that you do your work is a valuable energy that you can use to lend a boost to your magical work. When you say, for instance, that someone is a Scorpio, what you mean is that the Sun was tracking in the constellation of Scorpio when observed from our position on Earth. As the Sun visits the various constellations, the nature of the prevailing energy changes. This allows you to capture that utilize that astrological energy to accentuate your own energy flow.

Chapter 3 - The Astrological Sun Signs

From our Earthly perspective, each of the planets, the Sun, the Moon, and other celestial bodies move though twelve stations in the circle of the sky above us. At any given time, the Sun and the Moon are traveling through the twelve signs of the zodiac. The energy of each sign is as follows:

Aries: March 21 – April 19

The first sign of the zodiac, the time of Aries is a very self-involved, self-motivated, self-driven time. The theme of the Aries is "Me First!" and more than the other eleven signs, Aries energy is completely self-preserving and aggressively invested in personal position. The energy of Aries is resilient and recovers quickly from adversity. Use the power of Aries for magic in which you have to be strong and assertive. People with the energy of Aries are action people and rarely sit around talking about a situation rather than doing something about it. Use Aries for:

Defending your boundaries and pulling in your energy from nurturing others

Galvanizing your independence and faith in your own position

"Bouncing back" from an experience.

When you need the wherewithal to move forward aggressively and push past boundaries imposed by others

Safe travel

Taurus: April 20 – May 20

Taurus is the sign of creature comforts and pleasures. Taurus represents a certain stubbornness and steadfastness. Those born under the sign of Taurus without fail will have beautiful voices and beautiful eyes. Taurus is a very private, protective sign. Taureans have a very strong ability to "switch off" and retreat from others to allow themselves to recharge. Taureans do not react well to change. Taureans are strongly connected to their sensory perceptions and are extremely tactile. Use Taurus for:

Creating comfort and luxury in your home and environment

Protecting yourself and your loved ones

Resisting change

Linking up your sensory perceptions

Establishing boundaries

Gemini: May 21 – June 20

Geminis crave knowledge of all kinds and are very invested in their own intellect. They are swift-minded and their thoughts tend to be fast and fleeting rather than focused. They are innately curious and mischievous. Governed by the planet Mercury, Geminis are communicators and are normally either very chatty or are prolific writers. They are often bi-lingual. Geminis enjoy seeing life, commerce and interpersonal relationships as a game to be won. Many Geminis are challenged in truth-telling and interestingly, are not usually very good at it. Use Gemini for:

Situations where you need to think on your feet

Taking an exam or test of some kind

Speaking in public

Discovering hidden information

Making money

Cancer: June 21 – July 22

Ruled by the Moon, Cancer is a very emotionally based sign. Cancereans are enormously devoted to friends and family, but can often not realize when their behavior or words comes off as hurtful. Cancer is a shifting and changeable sign, going through phases of emotion just as the Moon goes through its own phases. The energy of Cancer is very adaptable to change. Cancers are the biggest romantics in the zodiac and excel at making their partners feel happy and loved, but are devastated when relationships fail. Cancers are tremendously connected to their opposite gender parent. Cancers are creative and innovative. They feel deeply and are the personification of the phrase, "Still water runs deep." Use Cancer for:

Romance

Creating positive family connections

Matters of an emotional issue

Adjusting to change or adapting to a current situation

Fertility

Leo: July 23 – August 22

Leo tends to be a very lucky sign overall and they love being in the limelight. Lions are unbelievably faithful, but when a relationship is over, they cut ties and walk away. Once trust is broken for a Leo, there is no going back. Leos can sometimes seem clingy in their desire for attention and they prefer to be the focus of adoration at all times. Leos are trailblazers, trendsetters and leaders who are always up for the next challenge and the next adventure. The fastest way to get into a Leo's good graces is by flattery and the fastest way to have them close the door on your forever is to criticize them. Leos are extremely charismatic and charming. They are usually very self-confident and self-aware, but choose to emphasize the positives. They are positive thinkers and do not normally entertain depression for very long. Use Leo for:

Luck

When you have to shine in a public situation

Fidelity

Peaceful ending of a relationship

Self-awareness

Overcoming depression and negative thoughts

Virgo: August 23 – September 22

Long maligned for being picky and overbearing, Virgos are given to a meticulous nature and are born organizers. They do not suffer fools lightly, but are actually caring and sensitive until they identify someone as a "lost cause." Virgos will shut down emotionally if a relationship does not support their well-being. They have tremendous faith in people and in "the process" and refuse to give into a cynical or defeatist attitude. Most Virgos exude a confident exterior, but this can be a cover for an insecure inner core. Use Virgo for:

Organizing and Categorizing

Strength in Adversity

Discernment in Relationship

Overcoming Negativity

Libra: September 23 – October 22

A lot of crazy people are Libras. The balance shown by the scales reflects that Libras are often walking a tightrope between the positive and the negative, joy and pain, hope and fear, love and anger and so on. Libras are easily disappointed because they tend to create unrealistic expectations both for themselves and the people around them. They take this disillusionment very personally and very seriously. Libras, like Geminis (both Air signs), constantly seek out situations where they can express both sides of their personalities.

Libras are given to drama. This energy can be extremely productive in business and they are often very successful in their chosen fields. They are charming and can win the approval of those who are in a position to assist them.

They possess a tremendous drive to be around others, but actually perform better when working alone.

Libras have to be careful not to undermine their own integrity and to not give up on their ideals, dreams and wishes prematurely. Use Libra for:

Learning to dream and to create goals

Projects in which you have to excel while working on your own

Achieving Balance

Tuning into the negative situations around you that you may have glamorized

Scorpio: October 23 – November 21

Scorpios are arguably the most direct and intense signs of the zodiac. They are very driven in their desires and are very involved with the concept of fate and destiny. Scorpios are immersed in passion of all kinds, power and fulfilling their strongest desires. They often come off as "know it all" because honestly, they usually do know it all. They are storehouses of information and share it liberally. Although they are so forthright with sharing what they know and what they feel, there is a certain secrecy to Scorpios and often, a lot about them is hidden, even from those closest to them. You can see the storm brewing behind their eyes when they are processing things in their minds. They are reactionary and expressive about their passions and their emotions.

Scorpios are very intuitive and a lot of their work is done on an inner plane. They rarely forgive and never forget. They are entrepreneurial and usually own their own businesses. They often wear a social mask and interacting with them can feel like a test you must pass by providing the "correct" responses. Scorpios tend to be wise beyond their years and very powerful. They know what they want and they go after it aggressively. Use Scorpio for:

Perseverance

Issues of Business

Knowledge and Awareness

Intuition

Passion

Fulfilling Desires

Sagittarius: November 22 – December 21

Sagittarians tend to be exuberant, life-loving and adventurous. They set a goal and work hard to achieve it. Dreamy and optimistic, the Sagittarian often believes there is nothing they cannot accomplish if they can only find the right combination.

Archimedes must have been a Sagittarius since he said, "Give me a lever long enough and a fulcrum on which to place it, and I shall move the world." The archers are happiest when they are on the move and they love travel and variety. Getting them to commit to one relationship is a challenge. They love philosophy and all media related interests. They are generous, fun loving, optimistic and very honest. They can, however, in that honesty, be tactless and then shocked that they have offended. They love having new adventures and exploring other cultures. Use Sagittarius for:

Developing an adventurous nature

Going after a cherished goal

Travel

Upping your "fun" level

Banishing negativity

Capricorn: December 22 – January 19

Capricorns live up to their reputation as being stubborn, determined and stalwart. They are patient and persevering, able to overcome tremendous obstacles in their quest for success. Much like their mountain goat icon, they plod carefully and surely as far up the mountain as they need to go to get to where they want to be, ignoring all discouragements and setbacks. They are extremely focused and innovative while remaining cautious and conservative. Cappies thrive on affection and seek out relationships that will tolerate their workaholic personalities, but shower them with love when they are available. They have a quirky sense of humor that sometimes springs up at unusual times. They are sensitive, loyal and great listeners. They are also good at brainstorming and problem solving. Use Capricorn for:

Problem Solving

Looking at things in a new way

Cultivating Determination and Drive

Overcoming Adversity

Aquarius: January 20 – February 18

More than any other sign, Aquarians march to the beat of their own drum (which no one else can hear). They are stubborn, but changeable and will insist that rather than being influenced by others, they simply changed their mind. Creative and innovative, the Water Bearers tend to get lost in their own minds. They can be judgmental and harsh and often do not understand why everyone does not think as they do. They can be very eccentric and their intensity is often uncomfortable for other people. Although Libras run a close second, studies have shown that more Aquarians are in mental institutions than any other sign. Likewise, there are also more Aquarians in the American Hall of Fame than any other sign. They are the walking example of the "tortured artist." Aquarius is a sign of "extremes" and it can be a challenge for this sign to fit in and feel comfortable with the people around them. They are very humanitarian and social issues are important to them. Use Aquarius for:

Creative Endeavors

Discernment

Social Issues

Distinguishing Yourself from Others

Pisces: February 19 – March 20

Pisces are often mislabeled as weak when they are simply extremely adaptable. Like the fish, they slip and wiggle and move until they maneuver into the place they want to be. They are also very changeable and have difficulty making decisions that stick. They are mysterious, alluring and often gifted in their chosen field. Like Gemini, they are often of two minds and are constantly conflicted about which way to go, which is part of why they have trouble making decisions. They sometimes spend so much time in their fantasies that they have a hard time remaining grounded in the real world. Pisces are very sensitive and easily hurt. They can become confused, obsessive and depressed when their image of the world does not match up to reality. They are great visionaries and very romantic. Use Pisces for:

Situations in which you need to be flexible and patient

Dreaming the big dreams and believing in the impossible

When you need to adapt to difficult situations

Creating a mysterious and alluring persona

Chapter 4 – The Spiral of the Year

As was discussed earlier in this book, there are eight key holidays throughout the year that were traditionally celebrated by our ancestors during the centuries upon centuries when we were an agriculturally based society. In our modern world, it is difficult to think of a world where an entire culture was based upon the success of the agricultural harvest, the fertility of the livestock, and the abundance of wild animals, nuts, and berries to sustain life.

The power of those eight holidays have been woven into the fabric of our DNA and our minds, bodies, and spirits still respond to them. In Spring, we want to be active and come back to life again. In Winter, we want to nestle with friends and family and share time together.

We call these eight holidays and the progression from one to the next, the "Spiral of the Year." While some see it as a "Wheel of the Year" that endlessly turns, we prefer to think that rather than come back to the same place year after year, we ascend, so we come back to the same touchpoint, but on a level higher than before, elevated by the lessons we have learned. While it is easier to think of the progression through the seasons as a "wheel" or "circle" since it does involve the same touchpoints each year, we do not want to always return to the exact same place as we were the previous year, simply moving around and around in circles without ever getting anywhere.

To aid continual progress, try to envision the cycle of the year as overlaid onto an upwardly ascending spiral. It still cycles around, moving through each of the touchpoints, but each step you take brings you to a higher point. What you do today has been the result of where you were yesterday and last year and ten years ago. Your spiral ascends ever upward and your past becomes the foundation on which you stand. If you were to, in theory, stand over your spiral looking downward onto it, you would see clearly the eight touchpoints glowing away around the edges, but when you look at it from a side view, you can see that the path is ascending, taking you to your highest and best life.

When nomadic humans began to embrace the agricultural lifestyle and in the most literal sense, "put down roots" by cultivating crops to sustain their village, they found that these were the dates that held within them a particular significance to the process of natural growth. Just as those dates marked the important transitions through the literal

74

agricultural cycles for those first farmers, so does it take us, the modern "spiritual farmers" through our own yearly progression of life. We can still follow this same cycle to "grow" changes in our lives throughout the physical year and harvest them in the Fall.

The diagram that follows shows the approximate dates of these key holidays/touchpoints. Each one has a name, as you can see. Four are based on the equinox and solstice and four are named for specific points in the harvesting and animal husbandry cycle. These are dates that are recognizable to many as being important astrological and agricultural times that have prevailed in usage and celebration through history. Many spiritual paths are drawn to these dates or times near them to share in the energy that has become indigenous to them as a result of literally thousands of years of humankind's investment into and usage of their power. Each touchpoint on the spiral of the year will be discussed in detail to allow you to experience a full understanding of its place and purpose in the spiral of the year and how the touchpoints work together to create our progression through a year of growth and forward evolution

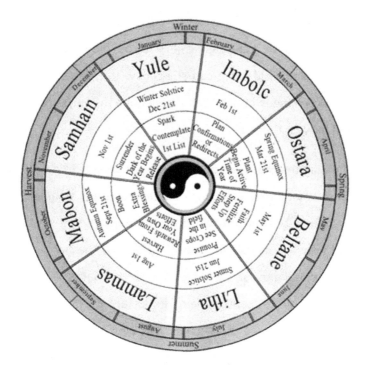

Winter Solstice

In the darkest moment of the longest night of the year comes the spark of light to the sky. Incrementally, the days will now begin to lengthen as the sun returns to the sky. Many spiritual paths see the strong, sustained energy of the Sun to be masculine and the Moon with its monthly cycles and gentle light to be feminine in nature. If we follow this theory, then this time of year is the most female and therefore, the most nurturing and intuitive. When the spark of light returns to the sky and begins to push away the darkness, we begin our cycle of the year with the "spark" of intuition and desire that will create the goal that we will nurture and grow in the coming months. Like the spark of life that springs forth from the seed, the spark of idea that comes to us now begins the process of harvest that will culminate in the Fall.

Winter Solstice Exercise: Pick a time when you will not be disturbed. Light a candle to represent the spark of light that returns to the sky. By that candlelight, write a list of all of the ways you want your life to be different by the time the harvest cycle ends on November 1st. Do not filter your writing and resist all excuses that come into your head about why the things you want cannot be. Imagine your perfect life and write out what you see. Distill the list down to a few things that are most important. Fold the final list and place it on your altar. In the coming six weeks, revisit the list from time to time, making any changes that you are led to consider.

Imbolc

During the six weeks after the spark of an idea forms in our minds of how we would like our lives to be different in a year's time, we solidify our plan and decide what we wish to plant for the coming year. The height of the Sun in the sky is noticeably increasing and so is its energy. The Quickening has begun. Now is the time to commit to that plan and put it out into the Universe as a solid and substantial determination. Once we do so, we will be shown over the coming six weeks whether or not this plan is indeed in our best interest. If we pay attention and watch for signs, we will receive clear confirmation or redirection regarding our plan. Sometimes, what we think we want in our lives is not what our Higher Self knows is actually for our own Greatest Good. Life has a way of showing us when this is a case and often we are suggested an alternative route. This is a time to be very alert and aware of both subtle and profoundly direct nudges and guidance that present themselves on our life path. It is part of the human condition to ignore what we do not wish to hear, but it is to our greatest advantage to be very honest with ourselves and accept the wisdom we are shown during this time.

Imbolc Exercise: Light a candle and then burn your finalized list in a fire safe place, sending it out into the world as your pure intention for the year.

Spring Equinox

As Spring comes to us, it is a time of new life and new beginnings. The earth has softened and awaits the seed that it will nurture and sustain in the coming months. The world sings with possibilities and potential. Having invested six weeks in the assurance that our plan is solid or else adjusted our plan according to the redirections we received, it is now time to plant our goals and begin the active part of the year. As ones who follow the natural flow of the year, we rest, reflect, plan and contemplate during the cold months and emerge ready for action when the first warmth of the sun touches the earth. By "planting" our goals, we begin the process of accepting them into our lives and signal the start of the physical actions we will invest into making them a reality. The Planting represents the end of the time of planning and the emergence into the time of doing.

Spring Equinox Exercise: Choose a dried bean or other seed for each of your goals. Plant each "goal" in a small peat pot of planting soil and bless it with a drink of water. Watch the plants as they grow in the coming days/weeks as an oracle of how the manifestation of your goals will grow over the year. Begin the mundane efforts of caring for your plants that will ultimately bring your goals into fruition.

Beltane

In many ways, this is the hardest time of the year because we have invested effort into the conception of our goals and they now feel tiny and vulnerable. After the planting is done, we may begin to see the first tiny signs of life emerging from our goals...or we may not just yet. An old saying tells us, "Do not dig up in doubt what you planted in faith." It is tempting to want to poke down into the planting to see if our goals are manifesting, but this is a time to step back, provide essential maintenance and allow the process of growth to proceed naturally. Fertilization occurs at this time with the seeds having been given a good start in life during The Planting. Now, we fertilize the ground around it, gently protect it from encroaching weeds or other dangers, water it just enough and wait.

Beltane Exercise: Get a confetti popper like those used at New Year's or cruise launches. Close your eyes and imagine that you are investing all of your energy into the goals you have planted in the Spring. When the energy has built to its strongest point, pull the tab and release the confetti and the energy into the world. Continue to care for your beans and nurture them. Now is the time to enter your second wave of mundane efforts into manifesting your goals.

Summer Solstice

This is the time of The Promise is directly opposite of the time of The Spark. The sun is now at its zenith and masculine energy is in full force: Do, Make, Create, Fix, Protect. The longest day of the year was a blessing for farmers as it gave them more time to work in the fields. At this time, the crops are very visible above the ground and although still young and vulnerable, they are seen to be green, strong and full of the promise of a successful harvest. In our own lives, we begin to see the results of our efforts and know that with continued effort, we will achieve in the Fall what we planned in the Winter.

Summer Solstice Exercise: Confidence is the hallmark of this holiday. Take a moment and write out a list of all of the positive qualities that you bring to the world. Look at yourself objectively and seriously consider all of the things you do to make the world a better place. Write them out and watch the list grow. Own your positive attributes and become aware of your worth in the world.

Lammas – The First Harvest

Although a joyful time in the cycle of the agricultural year, Harvest is also a time of tremendous, back-breaking, sweaty, muscle-wrenching hard work. It is a labor of love, there is no doubt, but it is certainly a challenging time. Many people find that this time of the year is extremely busy and productive as the fruit of their efforts begins to manifest and they are rewarded for the energy they have invested. The first harvest is the direct result of our own actions and our own efforts. What we have planted in faith now manifests in our lives and we experience the exhilarating rush of its fruition.

Lammas Exercise: Wrap fragrant herbs that represent your goal into two corn husks and tie it together with grass string or jute. Burn the stuffed corn husks as a representation of returning the first of your harvest back to the Universe as a libation.

Autumn Equinox – The Second Harvest

Historically, this is the time of the second harvest which was seen as an incredible blessing to the ancient farmers. While they were still pulling crops from the fields and putting them into Winter storage, nature yielded up another bounty that would grow with or without their efforts. As they made their way into the untended forests, they found fruits of the trees, bushes and vines. Nuts, roots, fruits, and other forms of food that were seen as gifts from God could now supplement their harvest. In our modern day lives, we often find during this time that blessings rain down upon us in addition to the fulfillment of the goals we planted in our own life's "fields." These are The Universe's way of telling us that we have done well with our year's planning and planting. While Lammas heralds in the work that we have done ourselves, Autumn Equinox brings miracles and blessings seemingly out of nowhere simply to make our lives easier and better.

Autumn Equinox Exercise: On Autumn Equinox, go outside into the night air wearing as few clothes as you can without getting arrested. Feel the cool, crisp air on your skin. Raise your hands up to the sky and say, "I welcome your bounty and blessings into my life!" three times. Feel the air begin to move differently around you. Know that your "boon" will arrive throughout the coming six weeks.

Samhain

In some European traditions, any crops remaining in the field on November 1st were said to be "poisoned" and had to be sacrificed when the fields were burned to cleanse them for the planting of the following year. Although we certainly know in this day and time that the crops would be no more poisoned on November 1st than they were on October 31st, there is still a valuable lesson to be learned by us in this ancient wisdom. "Know when you're done." "Understand when to let go, when to release." Even in today's demanding society, there are ways that we are able to take our hands off of the constant need to control and allow for a time of relaxation through the Winter months. The advent of November tells us it is time to do just that. This is when we celebrate the successes of our harvests and release our expectations for the things that, for whatever reason, did not come to us this year. Fields are burned away, cleansing us of the old and outmoded and encouraging us to release the parts of our lives that do not serve us and to fall softly into the embrace of

Winter when we will reflect on the previous year and wipe clean our slates to receive the new spark for the coming year that will present to us in December as the cycle begins again.

Samhain Exercise: Plan a Harvest give-a-way to not only lighten your own load, but also to allow your friends to come find their own harvest blessings from your cast offs. It is said that you cannot pour into full cup, so now is a great time to set up tables as though you are having a rummage sale and instead of selling, give everything away. When your friends have finally figured out that you are serious about this and have collected the items they want, give the rest to a charity thrift store and consider your fields burned off, purged, and ready to plant again when Spring returns. The truest nature of sacrifice is not about pain and suffering, but about gladly giving of what you have in order to make room for greater blessings!

In the book *CUSP,* we detail this process of manifestation in depth. CUSP stands for *Climbing Up the Spiral Pathway* and it is a spiritual path we have successfully used for more than 15 years to create positive life change every single year. We strongly urge you to read the book if you have any interest in a magical path dedicated to manifesting long term positive changes in your life. It is an extensive exploration of the very basic outline of the eight touchpoints we just covered and how they are effectively used in modern life.

Chapter 5 - The Power of the Moon

From the first moment that humans looked up into the sky, they felt an intense draw to the ever-changing moon. While the Sun offers us assurance and reliability, easing up into the sky each day and dipping behind the horizon faithfully every evening, lengthening and shortening the days as the earth moves around it in orbit, the moon reminds us on a more immediate basis that all things are transient. The moon rides its month long cycle, showing its bright, full face and then gradually turning away again to leave us in the darkness.

All faiths have been fascinated by the moon and most have included it in the fiber of their belief system in some form, either in parables, direct practice or even in placing the dates of their major holidays. Some faiths even use the cycles of the moon as a basis for their calendric system.

Honoring the moon as it moves through its cycles is yet another way of celebrating ourselves and our place in the natural world, as well as honoring the cycles that move through our own bodies and human lifestyle.

The phase of the moon lends the energy of the cycle of new beginnings, fruition, lessening, and banishment. The New Moon period is a time of growth and fresh starts. Waxing Moon is a good time to begin actions and work toward adding to your life in some way. Full Moon is a time of fruition and fullness. Waning Moon is a time to work toward what you would like to have leave your life and diminish. Dark of the Moon, which is the time of just before the new moon breaks out into the sky, is a great time for banishing things.

Nearly all goals can be phrased in such a way as to use the energy of the moon phase in which you are working. For instance, if our goal is to lose weight, we might be momentarily stymied if it is a New Moon. New Moons are for gaining, not for losing! We can, however, ask for will power, good health, a strong and vibrant body, greater self-esteem, etc. Working for wealth and prosperity to grow and turn around to banishing poverty and want. Just turn your wishes inside out to fit the Moon cycle!

Chapter 6 - The Moons Defined

Throughout the year, the moon moves into different positions and shows us different forms of her faces. The following is a traditional interpretation of the different moons that occur throughout the year and the energy that is available during that time. These moons are presented around the idea that we will be "planting" a major life goal in the Spring to be harvested in the coming Fall.

Cold Moon - This Full Moon occurs between December and January in the sign of Capricorn. The theme for this moon is "Joy." Winter is at its strongest point and is about to loosen its hold on the world, allowing us to return to a warmer, kinder time. Throughout Winter, it was often unknown who would survive and who would not. At a time when there was no central heat and when animals often became desperate in their search for food, danger ran high. Those who were not attuned to the cycles could suffer from "cabin fever" as they react to the limitations of movement created by cold, ice and snow. Livestock were vulnerable to the elements and sometimes, a sense of urgency for survival would develop around this time if the stockpiles from the harvest were beginning to dwindle. Reaching this Full Moon was a turning point that brought with it an assurance that warmer times were on the way. December gave us a heartwarming time to spend with friends and loved ones, being reminded of their value in our lives and sharing gifts as tokens of our affection. Coming from the glow of that familial closeness, our spirits are heartened and we feel our own inherent strength move within us, preparing us for the physical work that is to come.

Quickening Moon - This Full Moon occurs between January and February in the sign of Aquarius. The theme for this moon is "Awakening." It heralds in the first signs of warmth returning to the land and the sign of Aquarius gives us creativity, originality and awakens within us new ideas and new approaches to life. As the Earth quickens and comes back to life, so do we as our ideas begin to flourish around the new spark of an idea that will become our goals for the year. We begin to dream and to plan and to long for a new way of being in the world. The coming Spring can be sensed, if not yet felt, and this allows us to have faith in the unseen and believe that things can be different if we will them to be. We begin to build our hopes around the ideas and inspirations that have come into our head regarding ways we can change our lives in the coming year. We feel the stirring of excitement and a slightly premature eagerness to get moving. The

"Awakening" energy allows a clear understanding that our hopes and dreams can take form and manifest positively in our "real" lives rather than just live in our heads.

Storm Moon - This Full Moon occurs between February and March in the sign of Pisces. The theme for this moon is "Desire" as we solidify the goals that were born at Winter Solstice when the Spark brought the idea into on the radar of our mind. Because Pisces is very mutable and adaptable as a sign, the energy around this moon allows us to weather the storms that come into play as we receive our confirmation and redirects from God as to what to plant in Spring. It also encourages us to use the brewing storm of our desire and passion for what we are harvesting in creative and inventive ways while still remaining attuned to the natural flow and progression of the year.

Wind Moon - This Full Moon occurs between March and April in the sign of Aries. The theme is "Change" as the winds of change blow into our lives to prepare us for the planting that is taking place. As soon as the determination of what to plant is solidified, The Universe begins to clear the way and prepare our lives for the acceptance of this harvest as a reality. The Wind Moon sweeps clean the debris in our lives that would pose as obstacles to the manifestation of harvest and prepares our hearts and spirits for the change that is to come. Aries is also a sign of fierce self-protection and determination which helps cement our intent on the harvest that is to come and commit us to the process of manifestation of those desires.

Tower Moon - This Full Moon occurs between April and May in the sign of Taurus. The theme for this moon is "Perspective." It is a moon of complexity and contradiction, yet it works effectively toward its purpose of adapting us to the new way of being in the world that was ushered in by the Wind Moon before it. Taurus is a sign that relishes in creature comforts and physical luxuries. After the Wind Moon initiated widespread changes to ready the "fields" of our life for the harvest that is to come, the Tower Moon gives us the ability to find comfort in the change and accept that what appears to be destruction and devastation is actually working in our favor to ready the playing field for the incoming harvest energy. The Tower Moon gives us strength and fortitude right when we need it most. We often interpret change as "bad," but the energy of the Tower Moon allows us to settle into the change and prepare for the exciting ride that is to come over the busiest months of the year that are now upon us.

Strong Sun Moon - This Full Moon occurs between the months of May and June in the sign of Gemini. The theme for this moon is "Strength" as the strongest physical time of the harvest year is broached. This moon bellies up to the longest day of the year and heralds in the waning of the Sun's strength as the days now become shorter. The crops are in the field and the harvest is nearly assured. The sign of Gemini gives us adaptability and quick thinking to problem-solve on the fly and bring swift resolution to problems. The power of the Sun, in the most powerful astrological male aspect, is at its height and so the emphasis is on all things associated with male processes: strength, action, logical/practical approach and fierce determination.

Blessing Moon - This Full Moon occurs between June and July in the sign of Cancer. The theme of the moon is "Awe and Anticipation." We are now seeing the "crops in the field" and get a glimmer of how our harvest will manifest. The first rewards of the harvest are visible and that rewards our faith with strong assurance. Certainly, any manner of destruction could still affect the crops in the field, but we can see results and know that what we are doing is real and generates real results. Inevitably, there is always a startled feeling of awe when you first see the results of your crops in the field and know that the process is definitely underway. It is a time to celebrate our blessings and invest faith into the outcome of our planting. The sign of Cancer is very mother-oriented and this is a wonderful time to connect to Mother Earth and give thanks for all that Nature provides to us.

Corn Moon - This Full Moon occurs between July and August in the sign of Leo. The theme is "Gratification." The harvest is now beginning to deliver its very first results, which are those that come of our own hands and our own effort. Corn is often the first plant to yield fruit and it is celebrated in many cultures as the symbol of First Harvest. During this time, manifestation is particularly potent and can happen in the blink of an eye. In reality, during Harvest time, if you want a tomato, you go out into the garden, pick it and eat it. It is a time of instant gratification with little or no wait or process required for reward. It is essential, therefore, that we be especially careful in mind and deed during this time. The sign of Leo gives us great expression and joy in the face of the work required by Harvest.

Harvest Moon - This Full Moon occurs between August and September in the sign of Virgo. The theme is "Harvest." As the first harvest is being gathered, we learn how it has fared and how to put the early results of our harvest to best use. The sign of Virgo gives us organizational skills and discernment of how to use the harvest to the greatest advantage. The Harvest Moon hangs full and golden on the horizon and provided illumination for continued work in the fields even after darkness fell. It is a time of celebration and anticipation as the time of the First Harvest approaches a close and the second phase of harvest broaches. Harvest Moon can be exhausting and demanding as often the actions required of us seem to exceed the time and energy we have to invest. As the heavy Harvest Moon hangs in the sky, we are reminded that we are not alone and that our efforts invested into the Harvest are proportional to the bounty we will receive. If we do not go out into the fields and work hard, our harvest can rot in the field. Harvest is not going to walk its way up to our door and crawl into the larders on its own. Tremendous work and time are required to create a successful harvest.

Blood Moon - This Full Moon occurs between September and October in the sign of Libra. The theme is "Balance." As the harvest time slows down for the upcoming dark of the year, we seek inner balance for the adjustment to be made. Libra gives us balance and emotional detachment for objectivity and discernment. As the second phase of harvest dawns near the time of this moon, the energy of the blessings we receive come into balance with the overlapping results of our own efforts. This is a glorious time of bounty and we can begin to see that the end of the time of hard work and sacrifice is in view. The Blood Moon refers to the sweat and blood of our own brow and hands that we have invested into the Harvest and the degree of perseverance required to successfully and fully complete the harvest year. The balance is now coming into play and we will be able to rest as well as work as we begin the descent into the dark of the year. The Blood Moon is also so named because it was during this time that herds of livestock were culled and those who were unlikely to survive the Winter were sacrificed. The Full Moon at this time afforded a longer time to work at this grisly task.

Mourning Moon - This Full Moon occurs between October and November in the sign of Scorpio. The theme is "Mourning." As the harvest ends, we mourn the things that did not manifest and the things that were released during Samhain. Even though our goals are realized, we sometimes do not react well to change, even positive change. If we have been asked to sacrifice something in order to gain our harvest, it is during this time that we mourn that loss. One of the basic laws of existentialism says that "Every choice is bittersweet." If we choose vanilla ice cream, we may briefly mourn not having the strawberry ice cream. When we choose one thing, we inevitably un-choose something else. That is part of the balance that came to us through the Blood Moon. The Mourning Moon is efficient enough to recognize that as humans, we need to acknowledge and grieve the parts of our life that were changed in order for us to receive the bounty of our harvest, as well as the chance to work through the parts of our Harvest that may not have manifested for our own greatest good. The sign of Scorpio gives us both the passion to grieve and the resilience to recover.

Long Night's Moon - This Full Moon occurs between November and December in the sign of Sagittarius. The theme is the "Descent." It is time to welcome the quiet repose of Winter and the introspection that is to come. Sagittarius gives us the spirituality and insight to explore our inner selves and reflect on what has occurred and plan what is to come. As the Strong Sun Moon celebrates the most powerful male astrological symbol in our Heavens, the Long Night's Moon exalts the energies of the Moon, the female archetype. Rapidly changing and mutable in comparison to the Sun, the Moon hides her face and goes into seclusion for part of the month and beams down upon us in full glory at other times. The weather is cooler now, leading us inside both physically and emotionally.

During the dark of the year, we get to know ourselves better through spiritual exploration and understanding. Where the Strong Sun Moon represented the greatest physical energy of the year, the Long Night's Moon is all about emotional and internal strength. We descend down into ourselves and explore all of the hidden passages and dark, recessed corners of our psyche to emerge in the Spring clean, clear and ready again for action.

Blue Moon - This Full Moon occurs between the year and between the worlds. The Blue Moon is the second Full Moon in a month and since there are twelve months and thirteen moons in the lunar year, this can happen at any time and usually happens once a year. The Blue Moon is a particularly magical time when we slip away from the beaten path to celebrate, dance, drum and manifest those "one of a kind" moments. This is the time to make a special, ethereal wish and slip between the worlds into the time of the unseen and unimagined. It's a great time for asking for a special boon or blessing because the theme of this moon is "Extra" since it is an "extra" moon. Treat it as the joyful, magical gift it is and expect the unexpected!

Chapter 7 - How to Use the Moons to Boost Your Energy Flow

New Moon - New Moons are used for internalized work that often takes the form of meditation, visualization and relaxation exercises and chakra balancing work. We may also use the New Moon to start a manifestation process that will culminate at the Full Moon if there is something that we would like to bring into being. New Moons are a time of deep introspection and self-study.

Waxing Moon - Waxing Moons occur during the time between New Moon and Full Moon and are dedicated to the energy of manifestation. During this time, we create, build, and develop, bringing new projects into being.

Full Moon - The Full Moon represents "the full and completed result." Humans react to what they see and therefore, the Full Moon may be used either as a time to celebrate what we have received that has come into full manifestation or as full illumination to reveal what is hidden. Full Moons were historically a time of tremendous work because of the extra light they provided. Now, we use Full Moon energy to honor what we have created and to see what we need to see.

Waning Moon - Waning Moons are the time between Full Moon and New Moon and it is during this time that our focus is on what we wish to diminish or eliminate in our lives. As the Moon begins to get smaller in the sky, we use that energy to assist in the removal of attitudes, circumstances, and connections that no longer serve our greatest good.

Dark of the Moon - The Dark of the Moon is traditionally the last three days of the lunar cycle, just prior to the appearance of the first sliver of the New Moon in the night sky. During Dark of the Moon, the energy is best for scrying and divination as it is a time of tremendous psychic power. It is a time of stasis, rest, and quiet before the manifestation time of New Moon begins. You can see the inherent contrast Dark of the Moon holds in regard to Full Moon. Full Moon works with the external energies and Dark of the Moon works with the internal energies to form a perfect, complementary relationship.

By using an almanac or an ephemeral calendar, you can easily determine in what sign the moon will be full or new and what the sun sign is for that time. The attributes of those signs will influence the energies of that time and feed into the strength of your purpose for that moon phase. The Moon absorbs the same qualities of each sign as does the Sun as the energy attributes are specific to the individual sign an imbues that energy into the Heavenly body that moves through it.

How to Put All of That Together

For instance, let's say that the Blood Moon which occurs in the sun sign of Libra has a Full Moon in the sign of Pisces. The theme of the Blood Moon is "balance." We are heading into a transitional time as First Harvest evolves into The Boon and the Libra sun sign helps us to embrace that balance as the seasons change and the inherent energy of that time shifts. Pisces, being a water sign, is very mutable and flexible with change, so that allows us to bend in the wind and remain standing during this time of transition. We are also adjusting to the Harvest we have received and the new life it has generated. Our approach to the Full Moon could then be based around these themes of adaptability and balance. The influence received from Pisces is water-like and just as water always conforms to its container, we can work on conforming to our own environment and releasing our own expectations in favor of trusting what is there.

That embraces the Harvest aspect of the Full Moon, but what about the "working" angle for manifestation? What if you want to do some work to manifest money for your electric bill? First, it is important that you back track away from specifying a way that the situation must be resolved. It is normal for us to jump to a foregone conclusion that to rectify the electric bill problem, you need money. Not true. What you actually need is for the electric company to be happy with you. Your Moon work would involve focusing on the energy of the time, which is a theme of balance, mutability and adaptation. You could envision that your account is "balanced" and that you and the electric company be able to achieve balance in what you have and what they need. That then opens doors for either unexpected money to show up to pay the bill or for adjustments to be made on the part of the electric company to bring your account current. After you have done your Moon work, call the electric company and find out what kind of hardship plan or payment plan you can enter into. Once you have the definitive answers from them, going up the chain of command if needed, you will know the final ways manifestation could occur. Be open to any possibility. Once you have set the wheels in motion and followed through to the best of your ability, relax and know that the situation is rectified, even if you cannot yet see the results.

~*~

Thank you for sharing this time with us, which we consider a high-energy event in and of itself.

Blessed Be.

ABOUT THE AUTHOR

Katrina Rasbold has provided insightful guidance to countless individuals over the past three decades through both her life path consultations and her informative classes and workshops. She has worked with teachers all over the world, including three years of training in England and two years of practice in the Marianas Islands. She is a professional life coach who holds a Ph.D in Religion. She is married to Eric Rasbold, who co-authored the Bio-Universal Energy book series including the second book in this bundle *Days and Times of Power*.

Katrina lives in the forested Eden of the High Sierras of Northern California near Tahoe. Katrina is a hermit who lives inside her beautiful mountain home, pecking away at her computer keyboard. She frequently teaches workshops on different aspects of Bio-Universal energy usage in the El Dorado, Sacramento, and Placer counties of California. She has six children, two teens at home and four who are grown up and out there loose in the world.

OTHER BOOKS BY THE AUTHOR

(Available on Amazon.com)

Where the Daffodils Grow

The Daughters of Avalon

Rose of Avalon

The Dance Card

Energy Magic

Energy Magic Compleat

Beyond Energy Magic

CUSP

Properties of Magical Energy

Reuniting the Two Selves

Magical Ethics and Protection

The Art of Ritual Crafting

The Magic and Making of Candles and Soaps

Days and Times of Power

Crossing The Third Threshold

How to Create a Magical Working Group

An Insider's Guide to the General Hospital Fan Club Weekend

The General Hospital Fan Club Weekend Yearbook 2013

The General Hospital Fan Club Weekend Yearbook - 2014

Leaving Kentucky in the Broad Daylight

How to Be a Queen

The Real Magic

Get Your Book Published

Goddess in the Kitchen: The Magic and Making of Food

WEATHER OR NOT By Katrina Rasbold

Spiritual Childbirth

Tarot For Real People

Weather Witchery

Made in the USA
Columbia, SC
23 July 2021